Once upon a time, there was a
poor soldier. One day he met an
ugly, old woman.
'Hello, soldier,' she said, 'would
you like to make some money?'

'Yes please!' smiled the soldier.
'Then go into that old tree,'
she said.
'Inside, there are three rooms,
three dogs, three chests of
money... and an old tinder box.'

'You can have the money,' she said, 'but bring me the tinder box.'

In the first room, there was a dog with big eyes, and a big chest of money.

The second dog had bigger eyes than the first, and the third dog had the biggest eyes of all!

The soldier took the money, then he remembered the tinder box.

'Give me the box,' said the woman when she saw
him. 'That box is magic!'
'Hmm,' said the soldier, 'magic?' and he put the
box in his jacket and ran ...

One day a friend said a beautiful
princess lived in the castle. She was
unhappy because the king and queen
were bad.
'I'm rich, I'll marry her,' the soldier said.

But after one month, the soldier was poor again.
He remembered the old woman and the magic
tinder box.
'Aha,' he smiled, 'I want some more money.'

He found the box in his old jacket.
When he opened it – *Woosh!*
Bang! Woof! – there was the dog
with the big eyes.
'I want some money,' said the
soldier...

' ... and I would like to
see the princess.'
Woosh! Bang! Woof! – he
was rich again, and –
Woosh! Bang! Woof! – there was
the princess, asleep on the dog's back.

9

Next morning the princess said,
'Last night, I rode on the back of a big dog. I went
to a soldier's house!'
The king and queen were very angry.

The next night, they put a bag of rice around the princess's neck.

When the dog took her to the soldier, he did not see the rice along the road.

The next day, the king's men came
and took the soldier to the castle.
'Before you cut off my head,' he said
to the king, 'Let me show you
something.'

When he opened the tinder box –
Woosh! Bang! Woof! – the three dogs
ran into the garden and jumped on
the king and queen.

The king and queen ran and ran.

After that, the soldier married his beautiful princess and they lived with their three big dogs in the castle. And – *Woosh! Bang! Woof!* – they lived happily ever after!

ACTIVITIES

Before you read

Look at this picture:

What can you see? Write your answers on the lines below.

_____

_____

After you read

Read these sentences. Are they true or false?

1. The old woman is very beautiful.
2. There are four dogs inside the tree.
3. The soldier gives the tinder box to the woman.
4. The soldier wants to marry the princess.
5. The king and queen are very happy.
6. They put a bottle of lemonade around the princess's neck.
7. The king cuts off the soldier's head.
8. The dogs eat the king and queen for breakfast.

Pearson Education Limited
Edinburgh Gate, Harlow,
Essex CM20 2JE, England
and Associated Companies throughout the world.

ISBN 0582 344158

First published by Librairie du Liban Publishers, 1996
This adaptation first published 2000 under licence by Penguin Books
© 2000 Penguin Books
Illustrations © 1996 Librairie du Liban

1 3 5 7 9 10 8 6 4 2

The Tinder Box, Level 2, Retold by Marie Crook
Series Editors: Annie Hughes and Melanie Williams
Illustrations by John Lupton
Design by Neil Alexander, Monster Design

Printed in Scotland by Scotprint, Musselburgh

Published by Pearson Education Limited in association with Penguin Books Ltd,
both companies being subsidiaries of Pearson Plc

For a complete list of the titles available in the Penguin Readers series please write to your local Pearson Education office or to:
Marketing Department, Penguin Longman Publishing,
5 Bentinck Street, London W1M 5RN.

An exciting story adapted from the traditional fairy tale.

How can a magic tinderbox make a soldier rich and happy?

Penguin Young Readers are simplified texts designed in association with Longman, the world-famous educational publisher, to support children learning English and to provide a step-by-step approach to the joys of reading for pleasure. Each book has activity material, and there are also factsheets with Teacher's and Parent's Notes. The factsheets are also available on the website. Level 2 titles are written from a 700-word wordlist.

Series Editors: Annie Hughes and Melanie Williams

☐ 4 (up to 400 hours)	☐ Contemporary
☐ 3 (up to 300 hours)	▣ Classics
▣ 2 (up to 200 hours)	☐ Originals
☐ 1 (up to 100 hours)	

▣	British English
☐	American English

Cassette and video also published

www.penguinreaders.com

Published and distributed by
Pearson Education Limited

ISBN 0-582-34415-8

9 780582 344150 >

Cinderella